Rift

poems by *[signature: Barbara Helfgott Hyett]*

Barbara Helfgott Hyett

For Catherine Reed,
who came too late
to listen, but soon
enough to read.
Thanks.

12 Sept 2010
Worcester

The University of Arkansas Press
Fayetteville
2008

Text design by Ellen Beeler

The paper used in this publication meets the minimum requirements of the
American National Standard for Permanence of Paper for Printed Library
Materials Z39.48—84.

LIBRARY OF CONGRESS CATALOGING-IN-PUBLICATION DATA

Hyett, Barbara Helfgott.
    Rift : poems / by Barbara Helfgott Hyett.
        p. cm.
    ISBN 978-1-55728-865-3 (alk. paper)
    I. Title.
    PS3558.E4744R54 2008
    811'.54—dc22

                                                    2007044531

Rift

ALSO BY BARBARA HELFGOTT HYETT

In Evidence: Poems of the Liberation of Nazi Concentration Camps

Natural Law

The Double Reckoning of Christopher Columbus

The Tracks We Leave: Poems on Endangered Wildlife of North America

For my friends, of whom I have asked everything.

Acknowledgments

Acknowledgment is due to the periodicals in which these poems first appeared, some under different titles, some in different forms:

"In the Ring of Twenty Signs," *Agni Review*; "This Morning" and "Tour Guide," *Antigonish Review*; "The Arctic Imagined," *Big Ugly Review*; "The Chisel," *Brooklyn Review*; "Mrs. Noah," *Columbia Review*; "Late Love" and "Monarchs at Pismo Beach," *Comstock Review*; "Apollo," *Ekphrasis*; "Daphne," "The Talk They Give on Marriage," and "Sons," *Full Circle*; "On Earth," *The Harvard Review*; "Bravado," *Lumina*; "Life List," *Mid-America Poetry Review*; "Haywire," *Poiesis*; "At Hall's Pond," "Fists," "Rift," and "Vacation," *Prairie Schooner*; "Shameless," *Rhino*; "From Their Bed," *Salamander*; "The Barrens," *The March Hare Anthology* (St. Johns, Newfoundland: Breakwater Books, 2007); and "Hunger," *Reading Ruth* (New York: Simon and Schuster, 1994) .

I am grateful to the Massachusetts Cultural Council for an artist's grant in poetry, which afforded me space to write; to the poets of the Monday Morning Group, in whose company most of these poems began: Steve Ablon, Alan Albert, Susan Bazett, Hanne Bernstein, Jim Sheehan, Bob Thomas, Debora VanderMolen, and Alan West; to all the members of the Workshop for Publishing Poets, who have taught me, by their example, the tenacious discipline of hope; to the friends who provided the manuscript assistance, literary, technical, and otherwise: Julia Baron, Zora Berger, Poppy Brandes, Wendy Drexler, Cathrine Dysert, Susan Hampton, Grey Held, Carol

Hobbs, Richard Hoffman, Gordon Jensen, Gwendolyn
Jensen, Kirk Johnson, Robin Pelzman, Aimee Scorziello, Jean
Trounstine, Sandy Weissman, and Yuemin Zeng; to the col-
leagues who read the manuscript and gave me critical and
essential notes: Kathi Aguero, Ayelet Amittay, Deborah
DeNicola, Lee Dunne, and Sondra Upham; and to Enid
Shomer, editor *extraordinaire* of the University of Arkansas
Poetry Series, for her wisdom and her absolutely honest ear.

Special gratitude is due to Wendy Mnookin, my poet-sister,
who reconsidered with me, over years, every word.

I am further grateful to Maria Grazia Quieti and Bob
Sonnabend, for taking me to the Galleria Borghese, in Rome,
where I discovered *Apollo and Daphne*; to Judy Nadeau and
Eleanor Fenn Berg, who saw me through the personal process
of making this book; and also to the friends and colleagues
who provided me essential writing space: Baruch Roda and
Andrew Cohen, who built the "Would Shed" at Mason
Terrace; Bart and Marieke de Johng, of Montolieu, France,
for "Barbara's Place" at *La Manufacture Royale*; Freddy and
Betty Frankel and Kate Rogers, for sanctuary at their gracious
homes on Cape Cod; and Peter Bennett Speck, who flew me
to his flat on the coast of England, so that I could gather and
revise the many drafts.

I would not have written this book without the love, respect,
and encouragement of my sons, Brian and Eric, and my
daughter-in-law, Amy, nor would this book be what it is with-
out the joy of new grandchildren, Kayla and Jedidiah, who
have secured a future for us all.

Contents

Three: The Flesh

Four: Dura Mater

. . . We can so easily
slip back from what we have struggled to attain,
abruptly, into a life we never wanted—

—Rilke

Rift

one

The Ring

From Their Bed

He rises slowly, so as
not to wake her. An ox is
that careful as it tears the grasses,
consumes the tenderness beneath
the stem. He dresses in the closet,
as if she did not see his thighs
tucked quickly into the privacy
of pants. She stays awhile, half-
sleeping, the sun on the sill
collecting itself like the man
he meant to be—
singular, unharmed by love.

Whose

Day rises like a carp from water.
Whose net is waiting, whose
eye ready to seize what breaks
the surface, whose hand dipped in?
Whose shadow stipples street light
on the sidewalk? Whose flesh
bristles, and in that interval, whose
cools from the blush? Who pulls
the shade on darkness? Whose door
slammed shut? Whose voice is
willing? Whose sweat? Whose stain?

The Children

It is winter. There are children
sleeping. She has unrolled their socks,
set them on the radiator as a surprise.
She blows her breath into those socks
to wake their feet. She will love those
children, come from her body steaming.
She is to them a house.
They feed there.

So pretty they are, long-lashed,
tender-hearted
as snails. The youngest drums
two spoons on the kitchen table.
The firstborn
tears a paper napkin into shreds.

They stare into their bowls
of oatmeal, and they eat. *Slowly. Slowly*,
the milk already spilled.

His Gifts

She didn't want them: too many.
And too much. Why, then,
the breathy *thank you's*, the sexy,
slow unwrappings, her tying
the red silk ribbons in her hair?
He flattered her with antique
lacy valentines, Madame Rochas
perfume, peignoirs, and chocolate,
a leather-bound volume of Baudelaire—
ruse of substitutions!
When she was
pregnant, he went out in the night
to buy her a bag of Oreos, craved
wildly. She tore that bag open, ate
all the halves with icing first.

The Talk They Give on Marriage

They seem so sure of themselves:
the sun streaming behind them,
the students nodding like swans
in a nervous circle. They fell
in love slow dancing. He didn't
take her home. For years
they broke up every summer.

The students lean toward them
like ferns. *Do you believe
in one true love?*
No, they say
as one. *What do you do when
you get bored with one another?*
Hotels, they laugh.
When you fight, who leaves?

Do you have the same view of God?
Married is what she believes in, that
ardent litany, the presumption of comfort
and give. *Since you've been married
has either of you loved someone else?*
Yes, she answers. He looks away.
Have you ever considered divorce?

Oh, they want to know everything—
a girl begins to braid, unbraid her hair.

Mrs. Noah

She wakes to thunder,
the thorn of a husband's
leg upon her. Her body
has been his mountain,
his hillock, his plain.
She prays to the animals
in their untidy rooms.
In the forests of water
the animals are angels,
some standing, some
married to piss-soaked
straw. Din is its own
hard pillow. Her dreams
are stones on water,
invisible, small. She
has filled every bowl
to overflowing, as if
rain were a blessing,
as if the name she has
forgotten remembers her.

Vacation

1.

You don't worship me, he says,
eyes on the marsh, arms stretched
on the table before him. *I love you,*
she answers behind him, her palm brushing
his hair. *I want to be adored,* he says.
She kisses the top of his head lightly.
I love you, and now she is stroking
his shoulder. This very shoulder. This hair.
It is late afternoon. The beach still clings
to her thighs.

2.

At the bay, the minnows
seemed to kiss her, take
her legs into their mouths.
She couldn't count their see-through
bodies, blue-spotted foreheads—
as if they had foreheads. Spawned
into that instant, those tiny fish
were feeding. They were ravenous.
She was all they had.

3.

In the shower, she turns her back
on the tiles, refuses the soap, lets

her hair take the water in
and hold it there. She thinks
of his toes, their perfect roundness.
She thinks of the power in his hands.
The shower is careful with her,
her shoulders giving in.
All of her life is water,
and what she fears is water also.

In Bed, Reading *Moby-Dick*

The tension mounts. They grow
more and more impassioned.
They are in it for life. In it,
between waves and maelstrom.
One goes down, sings, unearthly
to the other. One stays standing
on the bow, despite weather
and the scale of his delusion—
he cannot disengage. She reads them
both into action, tensing, tensing,
smashing their heads together, each
in his portion: the whale, atoning
in water, Ahab's dark grief
torn open. Their world is conflated.
She can't sleep this close to what
she might, in loneliness, become.

Assuming Happiness

It is her custom at the mailbox
to be hopeful.
Anything could happen. Someone
could offer her position or reward.
Once her father won the Irish
Sweepstakes and the mailman
carried that amazement up
three flights of tenement stairs.
The mailbox is never empty, never
withholding. The dentist
reminds her it's her birthday,
scrawl of a friend—the stamp
on a Spanish postcard—tiles
of the Alhambra, so flamboyant!
The expectation of happiness
is happiness. She could be purposive,
and gifted, and destined for great
good luck: any day, except
this one, when the phone rings
too early—*I am the husband*
of your husband's lover—
any day, the unimagined thing.

Black Sock

Is it true? she asks him.
You slept with her here?
Peach striped wallpaper,
peach chenille spread—
He is wearing his
undershirt. He shrugs
—*No big deal!* She backs
through the door, and down
the hallway, maybe she'll
do some laundry. She shakes
sheets from the dryer when
one of his socks falls out.
She takes that sock
to her cheek. She lies
on the floor beside it.
She curls into a circle
by the wall. Fear is
a kind of obstinance.
She speaks to the wall. No
sound is willing.
Beneath her skin a bruise
is blooming. At the slightest
insistence the weight of that
sock could turn her
unsuspecting ankle blue.

Fists

She raised her fists and struck him.
She swung at his chest and he took it—
three blows. Enough to bruise him.
Then he caught her wrists with his
hands, returned them to her, gently.
It was a delicate instance, the way
he tamped down that naïve fire.

She breathed her hands, she breathed
especially her arms, the fine blond
hairs that grew there.

He perched on the counter,
boyish in summer shorts.
She lay her face on his thighs.
Breathed him. He patted her hair
with a hand. *Poor you,* he
told the top of her head.

His boat shoes were tapping
the cabinet. It was all
he could do not to run.

Considering Killing Him Instead

Something simple: a hammer.
One whack. A kitchen knife,
serrated. A kitchen match,
kerosene from the orange can
in the garage. The garden hose.
The garden itself. Those tubers
could do it if she trained them.
The fence post if she could tear it
from its mooring. A sidewalk
square, in pieces—too complex.
Then teeth that grind. Hands—
nothing to mediate that blow.

Ash

His hands are ash,
hands of a shepherd, hands
of his father, and of his.

His hair is ash and ash
sparks from it: leaves
of ash perturb
the ground.

His heart is ash.

In his shoes of ash
he walks in ash,
and his face is white
ash ascending.

He is god
of ash, and of
the garden.
And the serpent.

Noah

Among the rude democracy
of wife and sons, he had
no words, so rankled he
could jump into the roil.
Sure he had to steer
the living world
from there to nowhere.
Just that he couldn't carry
everyone all the way—
such stench and steam,
cawing and plain-out
screaming in the hold.
By the time the dove
returned he didn't want it,
pitched it over, rowed on.
He'll make a sweet story
to cover this,
which is so often
the case when a man
loses heart.

Hex

The clams won't show their faces.
Tiny sea stars will appear. Although
he'll want to take a small collection,
the tide will make them disappear.
Another fisherman, long-legged,
flesh glistening in between
his rubber boots and shorts, will
get the keepers, while her husband's
pail will stay empty, except for bait,
and the bait will be desperate,
though he won't notice. *Only bait*
he'll be thinking. But they're fish.

Hadassah Bargain Spot

She slips from her finger
the wedding band, drops it
into the hand of the guy
with the Jesus nametag.
¡Madre mia! he gasps,
crossing himself, shaking
his head, trying to give
that ring back, but she
steps away, so he puts
the ring carefully down,
both of them staring
at it now, like it was
blood. *Gotta talk
to Paulie,* he says,
and clears his throat,
dials the black rotary
phone. So Paulie gambols
in from the back, worrying
why Jesus is half in tears.
It's OK, man, Paulie says,
but Jesus is wagging that ring,
pleading, so Paulie holds it
up to his own big brown eyes,
reading *TE AMO SIEMPRE*
inscribed there. *It's OK,*
she's saying, *he's a son
of a bitch,* and Jesus
starts raising his arms

from behind the register—
May rose petals fall
at your feet, he's praying,
and Paulie, nodding, practically
singing in a moody way,
Yeah! She leaves that ring
beatified in his hand.

Life List

He calls her for his box of winter
scarves. Tweed scarf they'd bought
in England, the silk from France.
He calls for his gloves.
He calls for *A Field Guide
to North American Birds,* their life
list he insists is his. She throws in his
mounted butterflies, the whale bone
from the mantel, his fishing tackle,
every rod. *Look around your mother's
house,* he tells the boys. *The only
thing missing is me.* The car is
flummoxed—she throws in the map
of New Jersey, the ewer from Crete,
his antique business card holder,
six albums of souvenir postcards
of Atlantic City, where they were born.
  *She kissed his fingers, she kissed
  his knuckles—*
he took the paintings off the walls.
The surface split—
  *She kissed the helmets
  of his knees.*
He took the silver. He took the bedding.
  Always. Forever—
He took the doorknobs and he took
the screws. He wanted
things. And in that terrible
wanting, he forgot.

The Blows

There was no way to warn them.
They would have to love,
have to drink from each
other's mouths, and lick
their hands for salt.

The hemlock was poisoned
by aphids, she lost the baby,
the larder grew moths.
Blows came that did not
fell them.

She slept on her back, ran
for miles—in circles,
around the frozen reservoir.
Time stalled. She found herself
accomplished as a clock.

When it was over it was not
as they'd imagined. They had
used themselves against love,
or in the name of it. They
suffered everything they had.

Resolve

Nothing useful is needed. No bed.
No table. Let wood refuse. I will
furnish myself, lie down on gravel,
lie down on sand hours before the tide
arrives, lie down in water so that
the weight of water will disperse me.
A house cannot buy happiness. I will
lie down in green, slip the nuance
of myself, become the satin figures
of dreams in their many disguises.
Night proceeds without my knowing,
and brings me in. My hands recognize
themselves and I open my eyes—
I will stand. Or be made of standing,
and work. I will sleep when I need to.

Haywire

The moon seems real
in its poverty: limitless sand
and punctures, night tearing
the sky into names of gods
and goddesses I see, or
do not see. I work on breathing,
let my feet be frightened,
toes digging cold sand.
No one will come to find me.
No one knows I have gone.

The Pleiades, Orion's Belt,
Dippers, big and little—
as a child I stood with them
as I stood with gravity:
Earth, water, and the blue
star I promised myself
I'd see when I grew up.
The blue star kept me faithful.

Let it all go haywire. Let certain
fixed bodies turn in the perceived
heavens, and other bodies also,
be slammed down, knocked down
to crawl on the world I am
bound to. So too, love. So too,
heartbreak, fingers tapping
the breakfast table, the beds made
or not.

In the Ring of Twenty Signs

The third ring is the future scraping
the present: what is next enters, closes
itself to the past. The fifth ring is
observation. The sixth, satisfaction
of what is known. The fourth ring
is worry, but that is naïve, short-lived,
a waste of time, which is the tenth ring,
the middle. The eleventh ring is pleasure;
feeding, but not gluttony, sex but not
depletion. The twelfth ring: love.
The thirteenth: love undone, unleashed
attachment. Rings six through nine are
marriage. The fourteenth ring is silence.
The fifteenth, desire. The sixteenth
ring, mercy. The sixteenth ring is true.
At seventeen you stand alone on the stairway.
The seventeenth ring is achievement.
The eighteenth gives it all away. Not
generously. Not regretfully. Just given.
The nineteenth ring is loneliness suffered
despite oneself. The twentieth ring is the moon
and all its shadows. Rings one and two—
these are the human, delicate and susceptible.
The first two rings are the eyes.

two

Apollo & Daphne

Bernini Explains

—Apollo and Daphne, *Galleria Borghese, Rome*

I set before you two figures: man
and woman. They are the doorway
you must enter. Do not resist
the spiral of his longing, the grooves
and many facets of her fear. Do not
absolve yourselves. On any hill,
on any night too hot for sleeping,
remember them. Take as your own
the geometry of their encounter,
this wild and physical. This hard.
How far can anything go without
breaking? I have risked my reputation
to show you. So love is confined
to marble, so love set free.

The Chisel

I had my way with her, telling her first
where I'd be striking, what part of her
body I'd mark and shudder,
which breast past whiteness,
which shoulder, which thigh. I told her
everything before I did it so that
she'd come to want me. I brought her
further than that first becoming,
when men tore her from the mountain,
before she was possible, before she was
spectacle. In the hour of her first
incarnation, invisible within that glacial
tilting. Nothing to express but absolutes,
and she, immaculate, not ready to begin.

Daphne

What then this milking, what then
this giving way, everything forsaken—
courage, the spokes of bones, my hair?
In the world of men, I am the font
of abstraction, another myth told small.
They have polished my skin past human,
forced me to run as an athlete runs,
habituated to endurance. Dust
flew from my eyes. I screamed
into the chisel's yawl, *I am here!*
This fault on my cheek is not a tear
as was intended, but a bead of honest
sweat. Beyond the firmament of matter,
a girl holds wet leaves to her ear.

Apollo

What is the purpose of flesh if not
to exhaust me? How else to achieve
the full extent of the soul? I run
fast enough to keep her before me,
just out of touch. This suits my blood,
depleting nothing. My hand is fixed
to her hip bone, my knee replacing
her knee; my thigh, her thigh. I will
torque her face to my mouth when I
want to. I am a god. No tutor, no
music, just stride. There is between
us an understanding. When I move
earth beneath her, she will shake
like a laurel, and be glad.

Ovid

He'd have taken her before, when she was
innocent of his attention, couldn't tell him
from ciphers on the tree stumps, the gauzy
fog. But chase is what my ink demanded.
I parted her lips—*Father, save me!*—filled
him with wanting, such emptying and such
refreshment, the Engine of Being finding form.
When he'd set out to find her it was journey, all
armor and grail. He'll never have her; she'll
never stop running away. They are meant to be
cordoned. What they do is not their doing. Nothing
defeats that mineral attachment. He did not intend
to keep her, just ravish, once, that wild
refusal. Now it is always. *Always!*

River God

I saw the overtaking, the sun's
sweating pursuit. I could have
swept her from earth mildly, flesh
of my flesh, saved by cloudburst,
or the violence of sudden snow.
But I struck my only daughter
mute, made leaves shoot from her
fingers, roots alarm the nail beds
of her toes. Bark swallowed her
sweet skin whole. She was born
elemental. I made her stand,
then, unmoving, insensate
in the old-growth forest. I planted
her. I made my daughter strong.

The Laurel

I suffer wildness gladly. There are
medals and ribbons. Men wear
my leaves in their hair. Some walk
with a mountain's shaved face, some
are tall as a door frame the forest is passing
through. Every one a saint with his sculpted
entourage: foxes and eagles, the best
of intentions. I am to them an open
landscape. Only by effect do I suggest
myself. My veins are windswept
by the lively world. There will always
be episodes, and sacks of olives to share.
If love arrives, I don't need it.
All of my needs are green.

Sculptor's Apprentice

I cowed the light, for months drilled
semicircles into their eyes, charcoaled
the verge of breath under their lids.
I could not stop trying to make what had
been done already come out right.
I had meant to change things, meant to
have every detail mean. But they refused
my hands, wouldn't be what I wanted.
So I draped the marble, put away my
leather apron, closed the shop. I was
just an accessory. They were as lovers,
equally frail—his hand arced as if to
pleasure, her thigh ill with longing.
Who will come to lick that wound?

Tour Guide

Love goes on and I am not included
in the frenzy. My work is erudition.
My life, reading and renewal: silk
garments in my closet, to keep touch
from bruising, so that when I move
through the gallery, I am a lily,
perfectly detached. I speak of art
to circles of strangers. I am the one
who tells them how to see. Without me,
they cannot comprehend the hands
that tore the stone. Hour of ascension,
hour of husky shadow, I am content
to know the statues as they are—
unable to dislodge their marble arms.

Woman with a Notebook

My tears surprise me. I want to be with them
in their simple faith, but they do not exist
on my account. If I could touch the bone-
cathedral of their skulls, they'd remain
unruffled. Nothing excessive flows from them—
as modest as sunflowers, they need only
turn their minds away. *Don't go!* she cries
out from the door of her being. I hear the naïve
strophe of that sound. They are as one
trembled line, perfectly wrought, the ache
between their bodies, sheer forgery. Life
lies in the sexual ravel—he is not.
She never was. I have come so far to see
this betrayal. The marriage has begun.

Two Figures

We are love incarnate, emblem
of constancy, oppressed by form,
carved up and left here, object
of our own bare unity. We didn't know—
how could we, turned on the spit as
we were, without heart, or substance?
The ones who exposed us are as air
that sweeps between our arms. We do not
feel their dreams upon our thighs. You,
who come to watch us, nod, half in
recognition, half in fear. You sense
eternity, but do not seek the key:
if we are only stone, then who is speaking?
If we are speaking, then who are you?

three

The Flesh

Taking the River

I will take with me the river,
zipper it into my suitcase
and be gone. Carry that water
into my life on a wheelbarrow.
Push it before me.
Drag it like a sullen child.
Home, I'll put the suitcase
in my closet. At night,
I'll open a window
in the country of my language
while the river in the closet
runs. Whenever I need comfort,
I'll move aside the dresses, press
my ear to that suitcase. From this
position, I may begin.

Bravado

Even homing pigeons get lost
on occasion. So it's no surprise
that I am lost
in the way a child forgets
the bottle cap for a game of scummy,
in the way a child forgets her lunch.
Whatever I need is in another pocket
and I've come empty-handed, to sip
from the canteen of bravado, my fear
whipped up like a flag. I whisper
to my knees—*Go! Run!*
I tell my legs. *Fly!* I beg my hair.
The air walks by the dogs on their
leashes, the lovers smiling. I smooth
my brow with my fingers, quiet
my heart, my hands holding one
another behind my back.

Men

I forgive them their thighs. They are so
muscular, so lovely and their legs—
would perfect be too unkind? Forgive them
the hair upon their faces and the razors
that scrape them raw. Forgive them
their necks, thick and straining,
their long fingers, their hands. They are
large, they are ungainly. Their worry
is baleful, their tears uncommon.
They have powers of force and cable,
powers of majesty and all the earth.
They work and make work cunning.
At the edge of evening, they return
with their lunch pails empty, the Thermoses
within them chiming. The door is open.
They come in.

The Arctic Imagined

Mornings he'd wake and call for me
and I'd come to his tent. It was freezing,
I tell you. My boots were fur and my coat
was fur. I'd wear my nightgown. Scott liked
that nightgown, cotton and long-sleeved.
I kept it on so he'd feel that cotton
against his nakedness and the shape
of me next to that. He'd have coats
on his cot, coats thrown over us,
and my hair was tied up in a ribbon,
if there was ribbon, which I think
there was not. I served under him. Oh,
yes. I was the south and the pole
even more south. Or was that
Admiral Byrd? I served under
all of them, alone as they were, each one
holding his sex in the morning,
before adventure and single-mindedness
overtook him. Before ice and ropes
and the shouts of men, he held himself
limply, whoever he was,
and longed for the mirror of me.

Hunger

And when Boaz had eaten and drunk and his heart was
merry, he went to lie down at the end of the grain pile; and
she came softly, and uncovered his feet, and lay down.
                                    —The Book of Ruth 3:7

Who can understand why a woman would
lie awake all night at the feet of a stranger?
She rests on her shoulder, all tide and riptide,
not floating, not drowning in dreams.

She rearranges shadows:
cornstalks flatten into dark
geometry; beetles glean dust
and silk from the psalm of sheaves.

He flexes his nostrils. He groans
like a thirsty orchard; his windpipe
opens for air, his feet barely grazing
the fields of her loosened hair.

She studies the bony equipoise of arches,
his vulnerable heels. The half-moons
of his toenails gleam. At daybreak, she'll
meet the beast in the caves of his eyes.

Her hunger ripens—she draws the back
of a hand across her teeth. The story
proceeds. A kingdom begins
at the delta of her thighs.

Shameless

I break bread for any sparrow,
tempt one to our table. The man
I am enjoying tries to bring one
to his chair. It is early summer.
The café is sweating. *Whatever
this is, why not?* We are silent
in our prolonging, order tea
in frosted glasses. Every golden
woman strolling the sidewalk
is half my age. The city puffs
and preens. A pigeon floats
to the ground beside us. There
are sparrows at our feet. I tear
a crust, so generous am I in this
instance, so kind. In his shadow,
the man is bending toward me—
*Would you
come to my room,* he is asking,
come and be naked with me?

There are plums on the table.
*If I don't kiss you now
I'll die!* Afternoon rides on
too quickly, everything spilled
and everything gathered.
He has licked my throat clean
of plum juice in his pleasant
white bed. His eyes are green

and his pillow smells of cedar.
I might be thinking *Thank you
God,* if I didn't already believe
in his hands.

Late Love

1.
The waitress tries to light
the candle on the table
but the wick resists.

Does the match forget
the effort to flame, the acrid after-
smell, the thin blue smoke?

He comes late, smiling,
gray hair drizzled with rain.
From this safe distance,

I watch him unwrap his long
black scarf—was there something
else I should have seen?

2.
Life makes up everything.
Outside, the moon grows
angry, and the tide of stones

brings in more stones, ten
thousand shards for the taking,
cup handles and failed bowls,

the sea's porcelain dowry,
ten thousand households
tossed in the pummel away.

The past is too full
of dishes. Not a spoon
left in the drawer.

Myth

No one believes it, anyway,
even when it lifts from fire,
and the sun falls at its feet.
That's the problem with myth.
People nod, or yawn, recognize
the human proportion,
but the Phoenix has to die
and rise, all day, all night,
wandering from pillage
to plunder, in search
of a bird of paradise—*No!*
That's a flower—a falcon,
then, an eagle, even a red-
winged blackbird. Anyone
who speaks the same language.

Be Careful, a Man is Breathing

There will be no deterrent,
though the sky is darkening.
An egret surveys the buoyancy.
I look back at the windows
of the city. You lean into wind
on the bow, the ropes untying,
the sails surging—what's left
of the sun is a wall on water.
You tell me, *Turn around!*

⌐

A man smiles up
from the alphabet he is
drawing in sand. His child
curls herself into the hoop
of the *P.* He bends to his task
with his whole, long body.
There is a kite. I kneel beside
a dog whose tag says "Harry."
I let him smell my hands.
*That black dog's got his eye
on you!* you tell me. Someone
has lined up Hershey's Kisses
along the tide line. We eat them.

⌐

The Leonids! What baring of fire!
We cry, *Oh, my God!* when they streak.

We shout, *Yes!* We kiss and clutch
the porch railing. We clap
our mittened hands. So close they come,
so fast we cannot count them.
Next morning, the neighbor asks,
What was going on up there?
And you laugh, so hard stars spill
from your raucous, ebullient hair.

⌒

It's your turn to get the coffee
and the flowers. Your turn
to bring God to the table.
Enough of your back. Show
yourself. Let me hear
that moaning. It isn't fair
otherwise. Come into the kitchen
and be cheerful. To hell
with your turtle and his fresh water.
Cook us up a western omelet.
It's your turn.

⌒

We wear gloves and parkas.
There is no season as far
as beach grass is concerned.
There is sun slanting, and
the waves arc tiny rainbows.
The beach we lie on is dented
with our boot prints. We kiss
until our eyes are sand-strewn.

You walk away to take a photo
of the skiffs and gaily painted
dinghies tied to one another.
A deer appears, staring at me.
I feel the weight
of that scrutiny.

⌐

Darkness rises. The shadow
of the hill is insurmountable.
If I long to hold you, I pretend
not to. I refuse to match
your stride. At dinner, our bowls
seem empty, though leeks and potatoes
fill every crevice, and your spoon
takes everything in.

⌐

Your face is flushed, chin
cocked in pleasure. The cat
comes to bed to read
our feelings. She walks
between us, choosing,
forsaking, choosing again.
Your lips are pouty,
the bedclothes, tossed unruly—
so callow, that disarray.

⌐

The cat makes it seem so
simple, so harmless—all night

long she considers the flesh.
So at home in the warrior length
of your hair, I can't tell
where her fur leaves off,
where your head on my pillow
begins. A day has opened
itself like berries popped
from the stem. Brave stem.
I will awaken your lips
by speaking.
A kiss would be forward.
A kiss, too much.

⌒

Ordinary toast. Strong
coffee at the kitchen table.
I study the headline—you
won't forget me, I am sure
of that. My laugh, for example.
My silk pajamas, for example.
My complicated mind. Card games
in bed, the books I read you aloud.
The cat, preposterously, adoring
you, obeying you—so glad
of the comforts. So private,
so thirsty, it took you
a year to draw yourself away.

Bodily

The wardrobe of love is changeable—
now red lace, now a veil. A worn shirt
turned into a rag. What trembles
the breath and slams the chest
is not easily

forgotten, not now, not ever—
an uninvited guest speaks
from within the body in a voice
too felt to deny. There were men I clothed
in the pleasures

of my body. Their yearnings,
their smooth and nascent
foreheads, the rough cups
of their chins. I kissed
their swollen lips, my breasts,

my hips consistently working
unseen. I was a puppet
of my body, a fuselage,
a pretty compendium
of working parts.

Weather rearranges wild roses,
tilting their necks backward so far
that earth is assured of longing.
I walk the cobblestones, the bridges
night throws itself upon, preceded

by shadows: blue-shirted hydrangeas,
the flush of swallows, the hands
of the men who have loved my body—
Good-bye then!
Just this.

On the Train to Rome

1.
The man in my compartment
is sleeping—his huge fingers
clench in dream. Two buttons
down from his neckline,
he claws the skin of his chest.
Out the window, a calm rain.
Leonardo searched the streets
for ugliness, uncommon
features he could carry home.

2.
Three women in a field of onion
flowers bend and rise, one holding
radishes in rough hands. She ties
again the blue kerchief holding back
her brown, long hair. She may be
barefoot. But any vision is
romanticized, so she wears wooden
shoes, happily, uncomfortably,
beneath the church's spire.

3.
My only husband is imagined sitting
calmly at the window. Thinking,
or not. Not waiting. Not hopeless

either. Does he lift his legs onto
the table by the couch? He drinks
a cup of coffee. Two. His cat
is thirsty at the altar of the bowl.
I deny this image nothing.

Harbor

My hair is wind, fragments
of water spinning off every
curl. Wave after wave
ascends, exploding upon us.
Our little boat is trembling.
I am laughing, laughing

and he, too, is laughing.
Coming about! He is
shouting and I slip
from port to starboard, neatly,
lean back to admire
his muscular arms.

Hard alee! I have lost
my hat. My blue eyes
are crusty with salt.
I wipe them with my white
linen sleeve, the whole
shirt soaked transparent.

All the boats in the harbor
are shining amusements—
Husband, are you out here?
I can smell your hair. Which one
is your new boat? Do you
see me all but naked?

I take from my pocket red
lipstick, paint it wantonly on.

This Morning

I wish I had tossed the roses,
rinsed the vase of stench,
soaped and scrubbed it clean.
That kind of end to it.
Not this chitchat
in the waiting room, our son
in the OR, again, being
saved. We too, again,
sitting it out, after years,
the same straight-back chairs.
You seem fragile, he says.
I cannot bear his beard,
his new, expensive shoes.

Kittens

The One We Returned

She was hard to live with, that small soul,
nervous, and so honest with uncommon
fear. She cried. She'd cower at her bowl
when I fed her, hide when called, run
when I forgot and crouched too near. I meant
to tame her with attention, absolute
uncomplicated love. My husband couldn't
bear it. He chased her down. Resolute,
yes, and unrepentant, he cornered her.
Broke my heart. Locked the cage. Still she
didn't flinch. I touched her face, my finger
like a friend between the bars. She let me
stroke her, even purred. Though I explained
this to myself, we took her back unnamed.

The One Called Truth

She came in shadow before my dreams began
their disclosures. I shook awake surprised
by burrowing beneath the blanket, thin
substance grazing the hillock of my thigh,
my shoulder, my chin, the press of her body
trembling upon me, kneading my neck where
she fixed herself, appeased. I couldn't see
what breath flumed the thicket of my hair,
whose mouth rooted upon me, taking salt

from the primal store. I gave what I had
to in human need, opened freely the vault
of love. Perhaps Truth mistook for God's
my throat, but I, who'd never pawed, nor purred,
nor suckled my own children, suckled her.

Sons

And I reached down to take them—
each one caught like a window
inventing light. Light set
them down, one by one,
years apart. Two sons
sunk into breathing and my breath
sank in the tearing that freed
them. I kissed those heads,
the firstborn in his fat
contentment, the wiry last,
who screamed until I sang.
I sang as machinery
whined. Both times someone
sewed my flesh, pressed
my belly until what was
still within was delivered.
I was absent to that
intrusion, only gladness
swelling and those boys knew
what we were meant for.
They played melodic fingers
on my hair. When their eyes
opened they found me,
each in his own time.

The Straits of Mating

Through an open door I glimpse
my son astride his lover—
his lover's back, the strong neck
as arched as an ibis tilting the sky,

blue bed sheet describing muscle
and thigh. Outside, the sound
of rain thrumming the trees. Hard
to tell what is rain, and what love

flinging the sauce of the world
back to the world as rain
cannot help but do. Somewhere
there are glaciers, and gannets

preening by the tens of thousands,
and roseate spoonbills in winter
mangroves, their fabulous wings
pink from shrimp. Things go on.

Especially shrimp. Earth swings
in a most peculiar orbit.
And the royal terns are marching,
marching. Even the littlest

sanderlings, thoroughly selfish,
scuttle the new tide, *in with it,*
out with it, grabbing
what's left them in the wake.

four

Dura Mater

Hall's Pond

If this morning would slip softly,
starlings in their iridescence, the grub
in its clinging, the irises gone by,
like sun upon sun—in that shush,
geese might come to stand beside
me. Ungoosably, one might lay
her blazoned head on my lap. Proof
of a kindly nature, the sun would
insinuate itself into the leather
laces of my shoes, pond water
bounding in the narrow wavelets.
*Whatever is detached is welcome
here.* The males in their brown
abstraction, the hours steady as dust,
and the preening gosling who swims,
so graceful on her own.

Consoling My Friend, after Her Death

Caroline Rigby Graboys 1945–1998

I pity the sparrow who has lost
her wing, punished by the god
of wings, bound to earth, given up
to painted altars, regarded
as a wonder, or a sign. I pity all
birds torn, gnawed while sleeping,
ripped gluttonously in the beak
of necessity, by storm or whiplash,
or sheer atrophy, like a white
moon at daybreak. The last song,
incomprehensible, the fall
from the highest branch unheard.

On Earth

The tulips stand, tall sheaves
in their beds, and here
are the stars, the moon
unbowed, full-faced, a girl
with eleven moods. I wear her
fear as a star wears heat, from
within and without her
knowing. I would be as
a light to her. I would hold her
tears on my tongue, but she
can't afford that opening.
No redemption then, just
to dump the garbage, save
a slug, gloriously striped,
who means to slumber
in the pail that I turn
over, flat on earth, hoping
that slug will slide out.

After the Suicide of a Friend

D. W. K. 1947–1997

Could I forsake the body
as if flesh were not
the boundary of being?

Job saw a whirlwind
and called it God, tossing trees,
sucking up houses, dropping
them in a drama too surprising
to call real. So God is
imagined. So the rope,
so the pipe on the ceiling
of the garage, that release
from gravity, that urge
to forget.

Sometimes a voice
on the phone can set it
going, that rushing
anapest of breath.
There is passion within
the ever-moving cells,
and the heart, which is
human, is only sometimes
brave enough.

Monarchs at Pismo Beach

Rad Smith 1947–1998

Caterpillars sleep through winter
in little closets they wear
like bark. Such sleep is dreamless,
and shattering, though they lack
a way to know this. Spring,
they harden. Blood flaps
into span. All day, at the edge
of the park, hum of their bellies
against milkweed, press
of dry, unsated tongues.
At night, they're a cluster
of themselves, crowding
the trees. They sleep like you,
dear friend, in thin air,
abiding the welt
of one another's wings.

The Origin of Armies

The rivers were certainly full
of fish, for why be water
if not to give, or a fish
if not to stir the water
to flow? Everything knew
its place then. The torrents
that rushed the beds, the rain.
Even in flood, the rivers
stayed. No force to defeat them.
The fish went on in the course
of living, taking in what was
necessary, sloughing off
what was not. Moss grew.
Trees bent to drink in that
once-ongoing psalm.
At first there were too few
to plunder; there was no census.
A tribe began: woman,
man, accidental child
surprising as the moon.
Jackals howled free of proviso.
Wolves as well, and bugs,
winged or crawling (whose brief
stays were well-worth noting)
moved lightly on their way.
There were graves enough
for everything to go under.
Artists made the first machine:

six working parts to punch
the eyes in needles, first bone
factory, honed in the mud
that would be France. It was
a baker who invented
History. He pounded his fists
on the dough-table, cast apples
in windrows, sugared the fields—
in the end, he stood resigned
before the oven. History
is too big for any pan.

Rift

1.
The first Tower. Beneath it,
where my son is, the subway
dropping him there. He is running,

thinking: *There must be a gunman
in the station,* all the people moving
like a giant sea squid, climbing

up from darkness, up the stopped
escalator to the street with its lava
of screaming. Rage of paper, windows

flung out and raining, blue
seat cushions of an airliner
falling from the blue sky. *United,*

he thinks. *What the hell?* he thinks,
running, as when he ran cross-
country in school, just turned

thirteen, the day he saw a baby
fall from a car, saw him roll
onto the Riverway, the next car

coming, the mother, blue-lipped, her voice
shaming the vindictive God: the same
God my son is calling on now,

trembling with the others
in the shattering,
from which he will be spared.

2.
From the hillside, an old soldier
has picked dried wildness—
marjoram, thyme—and cut

the olive tree, small branches
for the table. He lunches
on pâté, sausages

tied in string. He studies his dead
wife's crayon-portraits, the striped
parade of ribboned medals in their frame.

Scrapbooks. Postcards. A tape recording
of the marches of his war,
making of his life a little

theater. He has carried pain
like a saint into the forest,
torn thigh raging—

Let dogs come if they want to.
Resist! Resist!
Any century can touch that wound.

3.
No one can find the driver
of the black car. Is that he
against the wall, the body

in khakis and argyle socks?
Are those his canvas shoes? Another
man runs by, hands thrashing air.

*I don't want to see this. I don't
want to see.* The driver's
door has slid away. Headlights

hang from the bumper, transformed.
Someone has quieted
the woman. I count six bodies

in the van. The windshield
is the darkest thing I've ever
seen. A policeman asks me,

*Where is the driver
of the black car?*
I can't say.

4.
This is where it happens: envy,
the urge to own the orchard, to take
it from the farmer by gun.

One push and the world is roiling.
History removes the oxen, the wagon,
the day and its meticulous weather,

women in straw hats bent
to harvest rice—
a bomb entrenched beside the bridge!

Trees falling, trees standing naked
in fire. Daylilies and dragonflies,
ice beating their turquoise wings,

everyone screaming, the river
convulsing, a spate of shadows
where a city once had been.

5.
At the red light I watch
the moon rising over the Public
Garden, yellowing the puddle

of an oil slick. In the crosswalk,
a cop, slamming a man against
the black hood of a car, the man's

hair flailing, his arm wrenched up
behind his back, too far. Sirens—
and the light turns green.

I used to be the Safety
on the corner, my long arms
waving the signal to cross.

At night, I'd white shoe-
polish my first-lieutenant's
harness, spit, make that

buckle shine. By whose
authority has everything
changed anyway?

6.
God once pointed to each
creature, reconsidered, shattered
the invented world on a whim.

It was a cold dark we slipped
through. The mountains
remember sliding when earth

wasn't earth but gashes, all
the other planets flung
in a strange eclipse.

The wandering of mountains
is glacial. Percussive.
Nothing alive to hear that roar.

The entire proposition is wandering,
a galaxy of endeavor. On their backs,
our forebears pressed their horsehair brushes

to clay ceilings, signaling themselves
in the limitless unfathom: caves
garlanded with dots and dashes,

the negative outlines of human
hands. They marked walls with
a coterie of mammoths, herds of bison,

riderless red horses—*there will be
no dominion*. Every figure, discrete
and irreducible. We are glued

together from those remains.
When Science discovers
the matter, we'll be found,

half-swimming, half-
wallowing at the juncture:
clumsy, vestigial, the apparatus

of a God-forsaken plan.

The Barrens

Trinity Bay, Newfoundland

All is cliffs.
The sun favors the steep.

A few miles out to the horizon
and everything bends. Icebergs
run three miles an hour, south.

If a humpback blows, say, *Whale!*
If a humpback lifts its face
to glimpse the encrusted
edge of the world, say, *Whale!*

Across the chasm, the puffins stand,
not frenzied yet in mating.
They dive, and they return.

Cliffs wear away to sea stacks.
If earth ever meant itself to be
unchastened, it has failed.

Small Boat

At last the long work of grieving
is over. For there is no life after
this life I have lived in like a boat
for sixty years. Rode it. Let it be
pulled like a battered dinghy.
Stood up to rock it like a leaf
on the sea. Slept in it thirsty,
rowed it to dry dock, painted
it green, festooned the mast
with ribbons and scarves,
sailed it, refitted, out of harbor
again. Then I netted a talking
fish for the hold. In time, I will
dive off the prow of the small boat,
let my death come slowly in.

Even After

In the north, a moose has come out
of the woods to stand each day
by a barnyard fence, his muzzle pressed
to the neck of a farmer's Guernsey cow.
All around us, not hidden but bright
and comprehensible, dura mater
envelops us in our rooms as we
undress in the solace before sleep.
That half-injured moon over the city
stays, even after we stop watching.
Let it be your forgiveness. Stand
before it at the window in welcome.
Place your hands on the sill.